On The Road To Damascus
And Other Poems

On The Road To Damascus
And Other Poems

by Katrice Williams

Stabilized Mindz Publications
P.O. Box 12938
Stanford, California 94309
United States of America
+44 7909 948 455

Copyright © 2008 by Katrice Y. Williams
Edited by Agnes Meadows

ISBN Number 978-0-6151-9239-0

Photography by Sunara Begum

Cover design by Danielle Padmore
Interior design by Aptronym – aptronym.co.uk

Library of Congress Control Number: 2008900064

This book may be ordered by mail from the publisher or on the web at Amazon.com

*All rights reserved. No part of this publication may be reproduced, stored in a retrieval system, or transmitted, in any form or by any means, electronic, mechanical, photocopying, recording, or otherwise, without the prior written permission of the publisher.
Printed in the United States of America.*

This book is sold subject to the condition that it shall not, by way of trade or otherwise, be lent, re-sold, hired out or otherwise circulated in an form of binding or cover other than that it is published and without a similar condition being imposed on the subsequent publisher. Copying, reprinting or any other use of this text that may infringe on the copyright must be authorized via e-mail at katricew@stanford.edu or at the above publishing address.

To Elaiwe

And

My African Sisters that I've left behind

"And Saul arose from the Earth; and when his eyes opened, he saw no man: but they led him by the hand and brought *him* into Damascus…"

Acts 9: 8

January 5, 2008

Dear Reader,

I have chosen to title my first literary work, *On The Road To Damascus*. *On The Road To Damascus* is related to the Biblical story of Saul who was blinded by God en route to Damascus. He was blinded in order to abandon his mission with Caiphas, his leader who ordered him to kill all Christians disobeying the Judaic faith. In comparison to my own personal journey, I would say I was blinded by a similar light and challenged to find my way to Damascus, picking up what I thought were useless tools for my journey, in the end aided me to regain my sight and complete my destiny. For the past couple of years, I have been both disillusioned and inspired by the world. I have wandered through thirteen countries, mostly aiding refugees, children and women. I have found none of these feats amazing or extraordinary, just a debt that I have owed to mankind since my birth. I have tried to take off the cover of my blindness to find my true calling and commence the rest of my journey in full sight. However, I still found myself stepping away from Stanford University and returning to London to fill a hole in my life.

Thus, I have written this anthology in response to that void. I have found that many of the poems included in this collection are a reflection of my life, whereas others are pieces written after my travels, from the lives of others that I have met or are a product of inspiration. It may be difficult to see how some of these poems fit under the umbrella of *Damascus*, but upon closer inspection you may find that they are all a part of the road that I carved out in my short lifetime.

I've been influenced by various people on this journey and unfortunately I cannot remember them all; however, one individual in particular comes to mind and his name is Elaiwe Ikpi. Elaiwe has reminded me of the new generation that is able to regain the lost humanity in our present society. By teaching our children wisdom, love and respect we can create a world that is not rife with poverty, war and death, but instead one blooming with love and hope. I write this book for him and other children finding their way in the world, in hopes that when they grow older they'll smile with me and reap the fruits of a better humanity.

Sincerely,

Katrice Williams

TABLE OF CONTENTS

1	Adam and Eve	9
2	Give Me Something To Hold On To	11
3	How Do Fables Become Legends?	13
4	Fridays	16
5	Ahmad	18
6	Can You Just Be The Truth?	19
7	Armageddon	22
8	Kiss of June	24
9	Soldier	25
10	The Namibian Holocaust	26
11	I Can't Play Broken Records	28
12	First Root	30
13	16-year-old Bulimic	32
14	She	34
15	A Strong Black Woman	35
16	He Walked Away Holding the Fortunes of Our Futures	37
17	Camel Woman	39
18	The Original Love Story	41
19	Kaleidoscope	44
20	Dream Catcher	46
21	On The Road	48
22	Lessons	50
23	Falling	52
24	Can I Fade With You?	53
25	A Battle He Can Win	55
26	The Miao Women	57
27	Mongolian Ancestors	58
28	A List of Dreams	60
29	On The Road To Damascus	62
30	The End	64

ADAM AND EVE

Adam asked me when
I was coming to visit.
I told him, "Soon".

I looked to him and said,
"When you are old enough to love me,
Then you'll see me between golden blinks.
On the road to Damascus,
You'll catch me with shells around my neck
And cowries in my hand,
Because gold is too heavy to carry."

"When you play your guitar
And the strings get stuck,
Then you'll hear me
For my voice is the only music you need."

"On the road where the sun starts to set,
You'll see my shadow approaching
With the weight and clink of diamond-linked chains
Around my ankles,
Because brass fades
And diamonds last forever."

"When your voice can no longer carry
The worth of my song,
Then you'll feel me."

"On the road where the moon floats
And the stars fade,
You'll hear my tongue carry the lullabies
Of the children borne after us
In incantation temples made out of blessings."

"So will you praise the on high," he asked me.

I told him, "Only if you will fill the other half with me.
When you are brave enough to sip from the gourd,
Then we will dine in my father's house."

"In the north sky,
High above the heavens
You'll find me on the road to the

Tears that have claimed stars,
There in my hands you'll find
The crystals that have claimed
The eyes of mothers.
And when those crystals can't be filled,
There we can have a drink of seawater."

"When you are wise enough to claim me as your wife,
Then you'll see me with a bowed head praying
On the road to where the songs of men
Sway the women into new steps of glory.
Only one most high can bless the passing of joined hands.
There you'll find me at the foot of the hill
Where women pray for blessings."

"When you are strong enough to carry me,
Then I will breathe your song.
On the road where children blossom,
Mothers wait their turn in silence
To carry a seed in their womb,
And plant the flower in their father's garden.
There you'll find me patiently waiting."

"You will give birth to my children?" he asked me.

I answered, "Watch my ribs, Adam, there you'll see me live for you."

GIVE ME SOMETHING TO HOLD ON TO

I'm struggling to breathe with collapsed lungs,
They're refusing to move under the weight of love.
We've danced this song before,
And we still can't finish each other's sentences.
Perfect. Harmony.
Is supposed to fit together into two clasped hands
That don't hesitate to hold each other.

Our hands make their own beat to the wind.
I cry when the dust spreads,
Filling the hour glass until it's all spent.
Give me a warning before we fall,
So I can prepare myself when you leave.

Fate's belly is full. She's waiting to explode the truth,
I'm trying to keep her from giving birth to the future
I don't want to face. Not ready to

Give up the past. I want to hold onto memories
That have been spent on countless arguments,
Nights when our voices faded into the twilight of dawn,
Creeping up on us each morning
Until our vocal chords shattered on disagreement.
We couldn't walk away,
Defeat would mean we'd sacrifice everything we had
For nothing.

I want to believe it cost more than that.
Its value was more prized than gold necklaces,
Blood diamonds, tea parties and frowns.
I wanted to believe my life in yours was more complete
Than without it.

I wanted to believe life was more than arguments,
Quiet moments that threatened to snap the tension
With a force more powerful than our desire
To make passionate love on scolding beaches,
Burning from our skin to our souls.
Now our souls are bleeding tears,
Feeding them to the heavens to rain in the oceans.

Our fury is what pushes the ocean's waves
To the shores drowning everyone in its path.

Stop me from crying and take back the pain,
So I can buy back the moments, the smiles and the tears.
Give me a hand to crush fate's belly and start over.
Give me something to hold on to.

HOW DO FABLES BECOME LEGENDS?

I met a fable that wanted to become a legend.
He was a wino that believed,
he wore silk robes and ate ambrosia.
He thought he could dine in our father's house
With Paul, James and John.
He was convinced he was the next Bohemian monk,
Deciphering over a hundred languages
And predicting the future of
Every man, woman and child whom roamed the Earth.

He was caught in a translucent state of Winter Wonderlands
And chariots guided by the king's men.
To convince him otherwise would only release
A torrent of curses on the unsuspecting patron.
Passerby left him in his bliss,
as he watched fairies clench their wands
And tirelessly dream Cinderella a handsome prince.
He walked by street corners to see Rupenzal's hair,
Chopped off in yellow heaps of yarn.
He supposed she grew tired of waiting,
She decided to become a rock star.
He dreamed that Atlas stopped shrugging,
And John Henry was actually a small man
Without nails or a hammer.

The Bohemian monk decided to make the fairy tales real,
By channeling reality into myth and stories into present.
He didn't know that his silk robes,
Were actually tattered garbs of a wino cradling his glass bottle.
He was convinced this bottle was his child
who wouldn't stop crying.
He held his invisible son in his arms and whispered.
"You can't change death, you can only change time.
Your soul is hard to barter, so tell the devil you'll give
Him a dime in exchange for a dozen."

"A dozen?" I thought, "what can he possibly mean?"
I paused to see the old man rocking back and forth.
Instead of the fortune ball and psychic dreams,
He had only a dusty bottle with a few coins stuck down,
In between his vision that his fairy tales were real,
And people that stopped to give him change
Were actually asking how to sift water into wine,

Stroke a Lion's back, catch an autumn leaf during spring
Or how to move through time, so that the past life
Would be recycled to take away the present insanity.

I watched him sing softly to his son that time corrupts,
As he stroked the head of the glass bottle,
Coaxing it to wake up and see the sun.
He rocked until he envisioned himself back
Into a two-story house filled with a loving wife and children.
I listened to him motion back to the mantle,
Where the fire burned and stockings hung before midnight.
He lifted a portrait of his wife,
the two of them dancing on their wedding night.

They shifted through the starlight to pick three little children,
Patiently waiting in God's land to be born.
Their offspring were seven, six and three.

Their children all laughed proudly in the backseat.
On the way from town on the darkest night of the year,
The snow was falling and the children reached their hands
Out of the window to taste the snowflakes.
Their mother looked back and grasped their hands.
But what dream would have it,
So that this man's worst nightmare would become reality?

Only a cold, dark night on an unlit road,
Where the wheels wouldn't turn and the tires spun.
The darkness came to invade
the laughing eyes of three little souls
And the heart of a woman that he danced with
nearly two decades ago.

Now twenty years later,
He forgets his son has died.
Quietly wishing his first born to be back in his arms,
Like the first day when he arrived.
He wished that fairy tales weren't myths,
Dreams didn't become reality,
Or that God could take away his worst nightmare.
He'd taste raindrops and autumn leaves
with three little souls from heaven.
He'd grab them from their cotton clouds,

He'd finish telling fortunes to his children during the day
And hold his wife at night to dance.
He'd laugh into her neck, smile into her eyes
And pierce her soul with hot-edged rhythms and songs.
He'd sing and sing until he lost wind.
Then he'd take his bottle and capture wind again,
Just so he could do it every night.
But if you tell him that this wasn't reality,
He'd look to you and laugh,
Smile and keep on talking to his bottle filled with the past.

Just to please him, I kept on walking,
Looking for my way up a hopeless avenue of dreams
And down an empathetic road that showed
How fables became legends that lived on forever.

FRIDAYS

Quiet anticipation at noonday drops
Softly onto the hips of the child
Swinging the rays of the sun on
Fridays.

Friday's child loops Saturday and Sunday
From trees when church folks
Bomb their way out of their homes and find
Death.

Death looks like four little girls
In Sunday school, choir robes
With the twist and curl of sweetness, but the press of
Silence.

Silence is the truth of angry men
Who don't care about the innocence of children
But they all look the same on a
Monday.

Monday brings funerals and cries
Cries are turned diamonds in a mother's hands
And the sounds of closed coffins under Tuesday
Rain.

Rain pours on black suits and blue ties
Ties a torrent on the hearse that trumpets down Birmingham streets
Not quite understanding why so many are…
Lonely.

Lonely like a Wednesday is the middle of the week
But instead of hearing the key at the door
Or the soft laugh of her kiss, her father feels the
Stab.

Stabbed right into his vision
His vision that today she'd be home
Walking with a hand full of posies, but
Ring-a-around…

Ring-a-around the rosies
Pocket full of posies
Ashes, ashes, they all fall…

Katrice Williams On The Road To Damascus

Down.

Down like Thursdays would never come
And take away the ghost that now haunts this room
She roams looking for her body, not knowing it's
Buried.

Buried in the depths of sand and darkness
Under the hole of exasperation and racism
Racist cries from white laughter kill her existence for
Today.

Today is the first Friday of the month,
Repeated everyday of the week
Everyday of the…
Year.

AHMAD

A gunshot was heard,
Before the loud, screeching sound of Ahmad's voice
Like a radiating blast
An echo in a curved ceiling
A penny dropping in a silent auditorium.
Everyone heard it,
Everyone listened so intently
As if they heard their cousin peeing
In the room right next to theirs.
At three in the morning,
No one said anything
But everybody knew.

I always said, "I won't be the first to move,
What if he's still around?
What if he still has the gun?
What if he shoots me?"
He probably does still have the gun,
And he probably would shoot me,
But he's probably not around.

Everybody knows everybody
In this neighborhood.
We know who shot 'em
We also know why and who else was involved
But as black folks we don't go lookin' for stuff.

And for that reason
We'll lie in our beds
Creeping in our sheets
Scared we'll be next
As Ahmad dies on the streets.

CAN YOU JUST BE THE TRUTH?

Can you just be the truth?
The truth that swings from trees
And on branches by ten feet of rope.
Can it be looped around the necks,
of those who've suffered?
Can it be spoken in the limbs that dangle,
That shake with the soul's expulsion?
Can this truth tell us the names,
of those who cover their identity?
They walk around our lives in white hoods,
Hoping to resurrect the souls of the Confederacy
And instill fear into the Negroes
Who'd rather seek freedom
Than the metal of a gin fan
And the barbed-wire neck of Emmett Till.

Can you tell me the truth?
For in their truth they say,
"Niggers are out of place,
Niggers want to run amuck in Chicago,
Los Angeles and Harlem.
Niggers don't know what's good for 'em.
The only good nigger is a dead nigger."
Their truth resonates in the ears of Civil Rights leaders,
Deep South farm slaves and house servants.

It rings in the ears of Negroes who have no say,
For the right to vote was stripped from them
With Poll Taxes,
The Ku Klux Klan,
Lynchings,
Burnings,
Mutilation,
Intimidation.
For the right to vote was stripped from the Negroes
Who had no say.

Their truth was fear,
And long nights with nine-foot crosses
burning in their front yards
The long-awaited breezes of burning flesh
And the much anticipated broken oak tree branches.
Their truth is written on the pages of the Constitution

That still says they are three-fifths of a man.
In the pages of state laws,
That still say race-mixing is not allowed.
In the pages of hate manuals,
That still tell how to kill Negroes.
The Negro's truth was sung by greats like Billie Holiday
When *Strange Fruit* still tasted of sour apples
When justice was denied to the thousands of souls
Who never saw their murderers face a trial date.

The Negro's truth was written in the dust
Swayed about with the wind
Whenever the Justice System so desired.
The Negro's truth has never changed with time,
Has never changed with time.

Segregation, poverty and ignorance still runs rampant.
The Nation's truth says,
"They're given the vote,
They're given education,
They're given Affirmative Action,
So why do they still fail?"

The Negroes' truth is written on
other's expectations,
He can't write his legacy without political interference.
Can you tell me the truth?
That still pawn shops, gun stores and ABC please feed me
Alcoholism is still running our streets?
Can someone tell me why our homes are urban,
And theirs suburban?
Can someone tell me how basketball stars make millions,
But their owners make billions?
Can someone tell me how some Negroes are rich,
But their counterparts are wealthy?
Can someone tell me the truth?
Can someone tell me why our minds are sized smaller,
We're deemed ignorant,
Lazy,
Criminals, bandits,
Gangsters, robbers and rapists?

Can someone tell me that despite "increased spending"
Our schools are still poor,
Broken down and hood-winked?
Can someone tell me the truth?

Can someone show me how we're not strange on trees,
But strange in prisons?
Can someone tell me how Harlem,
Compton and Chicago have not changed?
Why we're still trapped in hells called ghettos?
Please, can you just be the truth?

ARMAGEDDON

For J'Nay

One night I watched a sea of stars
As I lay beside my lover,
I stroked my fingers across his chest,
Palmed his face into my hands.

He lifted me up to him,
With a look of apprehension and grief.
His laughing eyes stopped smiling,
As I saw the universe reflected into his glance.
I saw the pain of centuries fall onto his lips
And the genocides of past, present and future
Roll from his tongue.
He pronounced the days as though
They were already done,
He looked the cries of mothers into my eyes.

He said,
"What if Armageddon comes?
What if the world crashes into the sun?
What if the world comes to your doorstep?
What would you do?"

I looked to him in surprise and smiled,
"It can never happen,
Earth will always be our home,
It will always live and grow.
There will never be a day where we will roam."

He pulled me close and replied,
"What if the only thing that lies on the streets,
Are broken bottles and dreams?
What if roses no longer grow from concrete?
And Hippies stop dancing to Woodstock beats when
San Francisco streets ban revolutionary guitar songs?"

"What do you mean?" I asked.

He laughed and looked to me,
"What if poets stop writing,
Singers lose their voice,
Musicians stop playing,
And painters lose their course?

What if mothers can't bury their sons?
What if they stop calling their children home?
What if love cannot roam?
What if Armageddon comes?
What if the world crashes into the sun?
What if the world comes to your doorstep?
What would you do?"

I looked puzzled and confused,
"If Armageddon comes then there will be no love,
Hate will replace the hearts of men,
And hope as we know it will die,
The apocalypse will arrive to take mothers from their sons,
Rip daughters from their fathers,
Bear dreams into the Earth so they cannot grow.
Blood will replace the waters of our rivers,
Peace will roam the Earth looking for Love,
Truth will be sacrificed on the cross
With nine inch nails through its hands, legs and spine.
Minds will be tortured with the thought
That Love can't carry us home."

He frowned to me and said,
"What if the world falls to its knees at your doorstep?
What if its voice has died,
Its heart is weakened,
And its mind is broken?
What if it asked you to free its soul?"
I replied, "If the world fell to me and Armageddon comes,
Then I will fly to each of the seven seas
To sing them one last song before the sun is gone.
For then, the stars will die and the moon will cry,
The Great Bear will walk in grief
And the world will have no peace."

He paused and replied,
"Don't you see,
Our voices will be drowned by the dying sun,
And our eyes will float in the dead waters of New Orleans.
Your pen will stop writing,
Your song will be lost.
There will be no time to rest here,
No time to love me one last time.
So, what if Armageddon comes?
What if the world crashes into the sun?
What would you do?"

KISS OF JUNE

Behold the kiss of June that fragments weave
Winds entwine in and out of leaves
Leaving traces of their dust-filled home
onto the lonely backs of beat box strangers
Humming tunes and playing gorillas off jungle trees
Bellowed onto the hot concretes of ghetto streets
Flowers flying off into their hollow despair as
a lip-pointed touch from noon-day suns
Caresses the tips of their petals and
approaches with a kiss of death.

Behold the kiss of June that fragments weave
Utterly perplexed in sweat
Young boys become young men,
Galloping as champions to gain their dynasties
Proving themselves with nine-millimeter sticks
And practicing physics with metallic bullets.
What's the projectile of a bullet into his head?
Can we calculate the speed of death?

The heat has us frantic,
Blasting stereos, carrying glocks
No man comes wearing dashikis or running blocks
For the 'Back to Africa' movement has long been dead in
Subtle, young ears who want to hear nothing of…
Preaching freedoms, village styles
Or campaigns in Mother Africa.
So, no words for wild behavior
No wind for where the lilies bloom
Only his quiet solace on the touch of a full moon
Count his blessings,
Walk his wrath,
And behold the kiss of June that fragments weave.

SOLDIER

Soldier,
Will you fight for me?
Will you take me home?
Will you save my freedom?
Declare me free?
Can you stop the violence?
Save me from poverty and war?
Will you take my hand,
And see me through this fight?
Will you help me stand,
And see their country fall?
Soldier,
Don't you know?
They killed my father.
They'd probably kill yours too.
They blew up my mother
And killed my sister,
Dismantled her face
So she had no identity.
Will you bring me vengeance?
Dear Soldier,
Will you be my guide through this terror?

Child,
I cannot fight for you.
I fight to bring peace
Through the orders of a general.
I've killed thirty sons today,
Forty brothers yesterday,
Probably fifty fathers tomorrow.
Do you know I am a human?
Taking a human life?
I trained to kill,
I trained to fight.
Dear Child,
Do not ask me to save you.
You think the winds can blow away
The war lines,
But the only thing that blows here
Is a hollow soul taking a human life.

THE NAMIBIAN HOLOCAUST

I saw their faces, I heard their names.
In my unconscious state of sleep
I lay in darkness, unlit by stars.
No moon provided a glare over my being.
I lay with my face smothered in ash,
Flat on my stomach.
I was afraid to move or think,
Feeling the dust underneath me
Warm with the stench of Death,
Violently caressing my naked body,
Encompassing my flesh with flies,
Overwhelming my nostrils.
The insects wanted to feed on my brain
As they were already doing on my open wounds,
Their four small legs,
And large eyes scraping clean the meal
In front of them.

Soon I knew I had no body
Enclosed not by dust alone
The friction of other victims,
Rubbing against me to free themselves.
We were cast too deep in this grave.
The weight upon my chest
Too heavy to lift.

I heard foreign voices reach my ears
Through countless bodies.
I was in Germany's dreams,
Black bodies piled high on each other,
Slowly suffocating with each tick of the clock.
Death taking the last droplet of life from my tongue,
I felt the dual taste of love and hate.
Love for peace and the hate the Germans felt for me,
Singing two songs one for life,
The other for death.
I lay here hoping
In the next life we'd never die this way.

I closed my eyes,
Asking for death's quick descent.
I knew it would not be far off,
My black flesh burning in hell

As my enemies tried to bury their mistakes.

As I died, I looked at the boy beside me.
In his moment of death
I could see the white of his eyes
Rolled up into his head,
No pupils, only flesh
Without a name,
Just a tarnished face.

I closed my eyes and fell to Death.

My body can be found
In the middle of the Namibian desert,
Under piles of bones, forgotten names and souls.
Our graves were neither marked nor carved,
Waiting for hands to write them into the Book of Life.
We're left eternally in the shadow of Jerusalem.
Perhaps if you look on the road to Damascus,
You may find that we are the wandering souls
Trying to find our way home.

I CAN'T PLAY BROKEN RECORDS

I can't play broken records anymore
They fall into my hands like lost souls
Hoping that through the love I hold
I can mend the broken pieces back together.

They roam the Earth looking for love,
But I'm always the perfect girl before they find it,
Leaving me to wonder when the music stops,
Where will I stand?

I look to men to place the record on the player,
Turn the needle, let it scratch away to romantic overtones,
Bass beats that drum silhouettes through my soul,
Prance chords through my veins and string vibes
Through my arteries till my heart bursts with expectations,
That they'll love me.

I am only the warm arms
Sheltering their wants and needs,
but rarely the hopes
It'll be me they'll glide with to Zion.
Fitting perfectly into their Snow White visions,
I allow their songs to fill my dreamy eyes.
Their hands slide off my clothes each night,
In memories that I'll hold for centuries when I made
Love to the drifter, the musician, the singer, the poet,
The dancer, the swinger, the Lone Star and the cowboy.

I was tired of playing Westerns,
Always the Indian they chased after.
Exotic and dark my flavor drew them
To my tent like the subtle taste of rain on the lilies' leaves.
I opened my flower to the sun,
Only drinking the droplets of water
Before the cold winter harbored nothing but frost.

So my roots freeze, writhe and twist in the dirt,
Hoping the desert will be better than this.
The sand will be more pleasant,
Anything other than the frost that nips my bud,
Yet when the drought comes I thirst for their attention.
Drinking and sipping with each smile.
To keep them, I plead.

I bow to their desires,
Filling as much of their need as life can give.

I give and give.
Their need is filled, their wounds are healed
And they drift from me.
There's not even a song to remember them by,
Nor poem to say that they were once mine.
Only my forgotten lips
To remind me that this is how they are.
Broken records that play on my chords,
Mended by a song from a new woman.
She fills in the cracks of broken dreams
that their last heartbreak left behind
with a note on the pillow saying 'good-bye'.

I'm left with a little more than that.
I'm filled with a thousand Cupid arrows,
Breaking before they even pierce through my body.
Pulling them out in tune to the new songs
Another woman brings by.

I put my face in my hands and cry.
Jealousy has long wrung my body, so I stayed
Until she told me there was nothing more to envy.
I left hope and trust sitting in the park,
playing with children.
The thought of new life couldn't bring me back now.
And love has been locked out of my house,
Sitting on my doorstep,
Waiting to get in.

"Don't knock on my door," I say.
"For love does not live here.
She's gone and dead to me.
I left her long ago,
Spinning old tunes on the record
That just won't play."

FIRST ROOT

The first root began in a dream.
I sat on a park bench in the middle of New York
a woman sat beside me.
Overlooking the Hudson River
We dreamed that one-day
peace would come
gliding in a white chariot of hope.

It would settle on our tongues,
taste like the candy canes in bedtime stories
nurturing our buds into smiles.
We dreamed the water was crystal clear
and we could see our reflections
at the bottom
slanted and childlike
just as the bent light made us.

We held hands
and sat in tears.
Our people were still murdered,
dead at the bottom
of not just this water,
but many rivers and oceans.

I flew from that dream
To the second root that carried me
into the arms of an old man
who rocked me like a father I never had.

He was one of my lost Cherokee ancestors,
coming to Earth to heal me of my pain,
guiding my hands to the clay that would
sculpt humanity from the shattered vase
to the bare elements of the Earth,
where we returned naked and pure.

Naked we would stand before our mother,
as pure as the first life
and as angelic as the last.
I dreamed with him that over a million hands
Would stand around the Circle of Life
Trying to catch the last beautiful breath of man,

to give our children a new start,
devoid of tears, pain and death.

We dreamed that the rivers would stop crying,
the clouds would stop hiding the sun,
the rain would stop salting the oceans,
the skies would finally fall to the sunrise
And a new day would approach when we lived again.

I dreamed he rocked me back to the Hudson River,
With the woman that held my hand.
She promised me that the sunset wasn't just for today,
And that our roots and dreams hadn't died yesterday,
They were things that could last forever,
As long as we remembered humanity just as it was.

16-YEAR-OLD BULIMIC

She's 16, thin, tall.
Her hair is fading,
Collarbone protruding from her shoulders,
Eyes squared into her head.
Food is a delicacy
To be looked at, not eaten.
Her plates are always half-empty.
She prefers to think that plates are half-full.
Greedy people fill their plates;
Sane people eat sparsely, even though they have enough.
Today she has pills.
Diet pills. Sleeping pills.
Metabolism-boosting pills. Hair-loss pills.
Midol. Tylenol. Excedrin. Centrium. Iron tablets.
Pills.
She opens the bottles,
Removes the cotton, pulls out one, two or three.
Pops them in like M&Ms.
Sips a little water and sleeps.
When she wakes up,
She's still alive.
Breathes, pops a couple of more.
Her hair is fading.
Slides the scissors across her wrists,
No blood, just scratches. Painful.
She goes into the kitchen and eats.
A leg of chicken,
A bowl of potato salad, a slice of bread,
A glass of juice, a cup of coffee,
A candy bar, a plate of collard greens,
A morsel of double-chocolate chip cake,
A pan of cookies.
She sits down at the dinner table.
Feels fat,
Looks at the hallway, walks to the bathroom,
Locks the door, stands in front of the toilet, kneels down,
Vomits the chicken, the diet pills, the potato salad,
the sleeping pills, the slice of bread,
the metabolism-boosting pills,
the juice, the hair-loss pills, the coffee, the Midol,
The food and the pills,
The pills and the food.
She feels empty. She feels good.

She's achieved her task today.
Now.
She doesn't have to commit suicide.

SHE

She cried today
The same as she did yesterday.
She wiped her tears
And rearranged them below her eyelids
That made lined patterns along her face.
The ocean's waves slipped from her eyes to her mouth.
She prepared for the night that would engulf
Buyers, money and her defeat.
Waiting would not bring her answers about the night,
So she continued with her ritual
That she performed everyday of the week.

She placed on her stilettos
Carried her black dress from her closet
To lift over her head,
Fixate on her body.
Each hip was embodied and not one
Spot of beauty was amended.
She flung her long blonde hair
Into one tight and stunning bun.
She placed on her mascara
She looked into the mirror to hang
Her diamond, chandelier earrings
From their ceilings.

Her voice echoed off of walls,
And seemed to fall
Into a thousand pieces onto the floor
Especially when she couldn't hear herself think.
She closed her eyes
Stood up straight
And went out onto the street
To sell herself again
The same as she did yesterday.

A STRONG BLACK WOMAN

For Mildred Goldsberry (1927-1997)

A strong, black woman
A flower with petals
That flower may have a limp
The wind may blow it down
The sun may drain it
Of all life
But that flower will never die
Feet may trample it over
Little hands may try and tear at its roots
But she says,
"I ain't no weed,
I ain't no nuisance,
I ain't no child,
I ain't no quitter,
I ain't no cheater,
And I ain't no slap taker.
So I suggest you stop beaten me."

A strong, black woman
Stands tall
And bows to no man
Not even her own.
She delivers sons into this world
To become men,
Proud of what they are.
She brings daughters to higher morals
To take nothing
Even if it's carved in gold.
She grows old
But never weak.

A strong, black woman
Has three tones of voice.
Loud, louder and loudest.
She'll give you an eye in church
If you dare talk about her God.

A strong, black woman
Will never back down.
She will never turn away,
And sometimes will even
Have a gentle hand.

Her hand is three bricks thick
When it comes across your jaw.
When you hear that laugh
It's the angels singin' in heaven
When you see that smile
It's cupids playin' their harps.
But when you see that tear
Her deathbed is near.
She says goodbye to all
For her Lord never left her by her side.
That's a strong, black woman.

HE WALKED AWAY HOLDING THE FORTUNES OF OUR FUTURES

In the beginning of time there were two lovers.
One that held the fate of mankind,
And the other whose voice broke heaven's soul.
The first was sculpted and beautiful.
He surfed on the backs of blue-finned dolphins,
Floating on the foam of the aquamarine waves
He blended the sunset into our midst.
He plunged onto the beach,
Clasped his hands together,
Shattered the coals of the dark mines
And forged the first black beauty of the Earth.
Taking his black champion,
He galloped to the sea
And watched the beginning of the sunrise.

Out of the blue the clouds broke.
The waves jumped into the air of flying fish,
Creating the first woman to appear before his eyes.
"Come forth," he said.
Grabbing her hand it was the dark silk of heaven's worth.
Her dread-locked hair fell back onto the sands,
And left a trail of clams behind her.
She held the taste of pink roses that bloomed in winter,
On her lips as he kissed her.
She lifted her hands to his face,
Painting their future for unseeing eyes.

Centuries would pass before men,
Created a shrine in her honor.
At its base some men would find gold
And others coal to continue burning the Earth's fire.
But she was always honest.
Her black-sculpted king sought the truth.

But little did he know,
That what he would acquire
Would result in the longest journey
than any man had traveled.
Looking into her he saw the future was
Brown hazelnuts that fell from her stories into his palms.
In her eyes he saw mothers' carved stones of oppression.
Women would worship her
For holding the smoke lenses when their husbands

Created fires with their fury.
They'd pray to her to bring rain,
Squashing the fists that bruised their consciences.
Still the wind would break through their homes and spread the fire.

On this journey her lover should have found,
Women worshipped her and
men pleaded to know her secrets.
Blinded by her beauty
her lover was distracted from his journey.
She tried to remind him of his destiny.

In anger, he grabbed his black stallion.
He wandered day and night looking for his path.
He made rain droplets to nourish the seeds for harvest.
He sharpened the rays for sunlight
to strike the laughing chords in children.

He even gave Atlas his strength ,
By showing him how to lift the world
Onto his back and throwing it into the universe.
Finally, he called out to the wolf
To lead him home by the moon.
He approached under the night sky.
She found that despite his search
he still had not found his way.

Frustrated by this revelation,
He placed her messages at the bottom of her shrines
For the multitudes to feast on centuries later.
He promised he'd only return until he found the answer.
The strange rider took off on the waves
back into the sunset.
Her sorrow was so great
she planted herself at the bottom of the redwood.

Hunters in the forests have sometimes,
Seen a woman dancing on the leaves.
Night watchers have seen the shape
Of a man in the sky.
If you watch the eclipse,
You may see two lovers meet
On the road to Damascus.

CAMEL WOMAN

She dances through the eye of the needle
To follow the camel into the Sahara desert.
She flickers dust into the eyes of nomads,
Turns around and caresses the sari dancers' feet
So they can flow to the music
That courses through their veins.

She is the spirit of the desert,
The ghost that expands the boundaries
Of dust into our homes.
We cough her essence into our lungs
As we labor deep in the oil fields.
Desperate to burn, burn, burn our souls
In the heat under the sun.
We see the trucks go by loaded with our black gold.
Our eyes pass slowly at the worker's faces.
We watch intently,
As watching is all we can do.

We look down to our hands,
And work.
Work until our labor bends our backs,
Until our smiles are gone,
Until the only woman who can hear us is…
The desert woman.
When the oil comes from the Earth,
She becomes angry,
Spreads the desert.
She warns us,
That carrying, burning and dancing on her boundaries
Will only bring more of the dust that fills our lungs.

"Sketch the lines of Nigeria," she says.
"Draw them so you people will remember this land is free
Free to all who nourish and replenish the Earth.
Free to all who will dance with me.
Free so we won't toil under the sun."

She remembers the land we toiled on for oil and gold,
The trucks that went by carrying us,
To work and work until the sun faded.
She cried when their was nothing left to carry from our mines,
She even watched as the Earth died.

I remember when the dust began to spread,
Our crops died and the Earth became a desolate plain.
Unable to bear the sight of unhappy faces
After all was gone and lost,
She danced back into the eye of the needle,
To follow the camel home.

THE ORIGINAL LOVE STORY

I look quietly beyond his hands,
Caressing the bend in my bow,
Realizing that love sometimes shouldn't be expressed
In the key of G,
But written in the strings of the harps.
So that when they are played it isn't lust,
Only caresses in lost hours,
When two lovers are forgotten by the world's light,
Remaining hidden on the dark side of the moon,
Trying to remain covered,
Wrapped themselves in silken sheets,
So that when the stars shine
They can't be seen.

It seems as though this is a love-filled lust story
Where they spend all their hours
Rocking slowly to each other's rhythm,
Joined at the hips,
forgetting that there can be two pieces to the puzzle.
Their hands know only each other's grip.
Their lines can only be written on each other's existence.

This is a story where lovers can dance
Without even holding each other close.
Where their eyes can look across galaxies,
Past eclipses and planets,
Through stars and glances,
Whilst not once touching the ground
Or letting their love fall.

For no matter through eternity's flight
Their love was the one that created the definition.
That this love story will last forever.
When Lari White sang,
'Always and Forever'
He wasn't talking about a shallow love between humans,
He was talking about neck deep waters
Lovers drowned themselves in,
To remain emerged in each other's love.

Yet something in this harp stopped half tune,
And they were forced to back track
To the roads they started alone.

It was a tale that shouldn't have been told,
A love so old,
It shouldn't have existed.
Hands held close,
That should've been parted.
Words unsaid,
That silences couldn't speak.
And days that passed,
That wouldn't become years.

This love didn't exist in the shallow hours of our lives,
Wasn't there when we awoke,
And wasn't a truth that we knew.
Only a fairy tale dream that we lived,
When Cinderella found her prince,
Or when Snow White went on happily with the seven dwarves.
These characters were only an animation of our love,
Drawn after we first expressed it,
Written after we first dreamed it,
Seen after we first pictured it.

We were the original,
Before time even knew it.
The Alpha and Omega,
Took a bow and tore this love down.
A love meant for Adam and Eve,
Not you and me.
She was sown from his ribs,
I was sown from your heart.

She began the first life,
I began the first stars.
She took the first steps,
I took the first walk.
She learned to eat from the apple and the tree.
I long knew that in order to be free,
You must first learn to live through love and harmony.
She has no idea what it is to give birth.
I was the creator, before she was the maker.

Adam and Eve were made from flesh,
You and I were made up of moons and stars,
Suns and galaxies,
Planets and universes,
That lasted beyond centuries.
Our hands created the first pen
To give the first poet his ink,
To write the love story that could never be written.

KALEIDOSCOPE

For Natty

So, what happens when great minds converge?
I can only tell you that as an observer,
With my silk-inked pen that they fly.

On the road, I wrote the chronicles of the foretold,
The song of a man that I only met once.
He sprang into my vision like a kaleidoscope
Does onto the mirror, each picture at an angle
From the other, diverges the lens, moves together
And then when you take away the colorful images,
The snapshots of locks, the smoothness of skin
And the mystery of the eyes, then you
No longer have a picture, you have a fading memory.

But from the picture, before it faded,
I saw thus a man, who I can only describe as a bird.
His guitar acted as stringed wings of music
That carried the rhythm for his vocals to dance into.
His hands played the upbeat wind for
My ears to carry his voice to the unknown.
And his eyes glared right through me,
As his song was the only vision he needed.

I simply was the onlooker,
The viewer in the shadows that stood
On the side of the wall.
And if the walls could cradle me softly
Again as they did that night
When I saw him fly, then he'd no longer
Have to sing about a woman
With bedroom eyes.

For she is already sleeping in the throes of
Wooden wing-tipped songs of locked seas.
Quietly cradling the walls of water that
Splash around me on nights when,
I remember guitar, string and fingers.
Fingers moving along guitar strings
As though they were stroking their,
Daughter's scalp or fiddling the sunrays
Into the oracle woman that predicted one day—
He'll leave this night.

He'll fly to the great beyond
That has crowds of voices singing
Prayers and candlelit vigils to his words.
He'll have to construct temples
To maintain the image of the Most High,
And contain the women that throw,
Their naked bodies into piles of steps
So he won't have to walk on water.

He'll never have to worry about falling,
Because hands behind him will be too cool for him to faint.
And the heat in front of him,
Can't out do his flame,
We can already see his inner core.
But I already predicted he'd be in metal planes,
Metal trains and carved up buses,
Carrying his bands, fans, posters and
His name on the side of the bus written in golden spirals.
Yes, I already predicted he'd be looking
Through the pane-glass window,
At the cotton fields and the woman
That pauses with her pen.
He might remember me as the girl
Who couldn't fall at his feet, but instead as the one…

Who outstretched my arms to the walls,
So they could cradle me to his words
And rock me softly to sleep
Before he traveled beyond that night.

DREAM CATCHER

Are you like me? Half awake?
Quietly contemplating in your bed of dreams
If I'm beside you?
Or are you half asleep?
Dreaming softly of a tender body next to yours
But realize its only cold sheets that
You're comforting.

Perhaps, together we could run
Half-moons around the Serengeti,
Naked bodies against the wind,
We'd roam like the lions do
And float like the call of the wild
amongst grass, plains and wind
that floats tenderly from the lost
animals to the silent Sahara
waiting violently for it to brush dust
on our backs and spread its wings
further into the fertile land.

We need not worry about the dust
Splaying its dry salt into the soil
And killing the crops of our children.
We only need to dream in states of half-sleep.
We could dream that we are nomads
On the hunt for peace and solace.
We hold our spears tightly as we crouch in the dark tundra,
Awaiting the bit of sunlight that will
Sparkle our eager bellies for the one time in the year,
When we no longer thirst for
The purity of melted ice capsules and hunger
For the day when the sunrise will awaken with us together.

See we roam from plains to deserts
To melted ice capsules,
Seeking our place in the Earth that can't be found
In story books, hidden passage ways or
Fumbled pages of Plato's Atlantis.
We bid ourselves to the ends of the Earth,
The bottoms of the greatest oceans
And in the core of the mightiest mountains.
Even the bravest warriors cannot trace our
Scent without dying of cold.

We brush against each other in half-states of consciousness.
Hoping that one of us will wake up
To find the other breathing tenderly beside us.
But we desperately hunt in realms that are too open
For outsiders to see.

Thus, we hide our mystery in our sleep.
Seeking and finding that in our dreams,
We are together.
But as long as I am here,
In the West and you there in the East,
I will be parted and bound to dreams.
But let the dream-catcher know
This is one dream I will not let go.

ON THE ROAD

On the road between somewhere and now,
Somewhere in the dust,
I lost all the parts of me,
They drifted off to find freedom
Leaving me to search the Earth.

My mind decided not to listen to my heart.
So, in a disturbed state without peace of mind,
My heart decided to run off with love.
Vexed and bewildered,
My mind went off in a state of confusion.

Somewhere in confusion,
Somewhere in the East,
My mind has wandered.
Disillusioned by my heart it flees.
My mind has the ability to travel across oceans and seas.
It's learned how to swim without a body.
So if you see her floating on a boat towards Mexico,
Tell her, she needs wisdom,
Tell her I'm still lost.
Tell her that love is not over.

Somewhere in the rain,
My soul decided to seek the sun.
She built the wings of Icarus.
Instead of wings of wax,
She built wings of steel.
No one told her that in time they would rust,
But still she floated after a jet plane.
So, if you see the smoke signal
Of a crashed soul,
Tell her, I'm still looking for her,
And tell her not to capture new wings of snow.

Somewhere in the chaos of my mind,
Heart and soul;
My body became angry.
Free of command she took off running.
Without a head she landed in the Amazon.
Perhaps in one of the stories the mind was
Reading, it heard that she had sisters.
Tell, her that I love her.
Tell her that there is a brother.

Katrice Williams   On The Road To Damascus

Tell her that I need her to carry my son.

If the trouble weren't enough,
My son's soul decided to leave me.
He floated around my head like a halo,
Waiting to be born.
In the midst of chaos and disorder,
He grew impatient.
Somehow Cupid was convinced he'd have more fun,
Throwing lover's arrows at young girl's souls.
So when you see him,
Tell him, I still want to hold him.
Tell, him, it's not yet time.

Tell him, I'm still looking.
On the road between somewhere and here,
My will decided to go on living.
Disheartened and dismembered,
My will somehow knew I had to keep going.
But she's slowly growing weary.
She's slowly dying.
But when you see her,
Tell her, she's beautiful.
Tell her, the other parts will return to me.
Tell her, it's not yet time.
Tell, her, I'm still looking.

LESSONS

I want to talk to you between
The time when the sun rises and the moon sets.
I want to be able to fill in the blank of our love's existence.
Answer questions
That have been dangling in our silences.
I want to stop waking wondering if you still love me, and not her.
To answer the question that there's only one of us.
I want my love to be enough
So you can let her go.
But somehow I know I'm only fooling myself,
Because you'll always want the better half of yourself,
You can't decide if it's her or me.
I want to wake up thinking this bed isn't half empty,
Your mind with her, and my mind
Wondering if she's still with you.

I want to know if you still have the will to let me go.
And I'd like to think my heart won't break if I decide to leave.
I want to believe we can fill our silences with star light
No longer remaining in darkness about how we truly feel.
I want to learn that through my words
Other lovers will listen, heed my warning.
Our minds are strong but our hearts are hard to follow.
We have to learn to love by walking away,
Not slowly wishing that we'd never understood,
Or asked why we'd stayed.

We have to want to sleep alone at night,
With cold sheets instead of a comforting arm
And only half a heart.
You have to learn to be a man controlling your wants
And I have to learn to be a woman fulfilling my desires
We have to learn that choosing is believing
That not choosing is deceiving,
That respect is vital, and love without respect is hopeless.

We should want something more than half-truths,
Learning that sometimes love, like doors, will close,
But new ones will always open.
And if we can't learn this lesson.
We have to live memories, not disturbed sleep.
I want to speak of the moment when the moon sets and the sun rises,
To tell you to speak of injustice,

Calling out the names of all your lovers,
The names of soul mates who could've been mine,
But weren't because I was too caught up in you.
I want to tell you how much I could care less about the world.
I'd give it all you, my life, my heart, my home just to be with you.
I want to say how much I love you
But I can't because I'm afraid the world might hear.
I want to go to places and do things I never thought I'd do.
Make love to you on each of the seven seas
And never drown, or think what ship might be passing
Or who might be looking.

I want you to speak to me
In that moment when the moon sets and the sun rises,
To tell me at that moment "Just walk away".
Maybe I could stop my heart from breaking.

I want this to be more than words, but a true story,
And all who've experienced this
to stop writing the 'happy ever after's',
Replace them with real life dramas, stop all the love stories,
Tell you what's real is only known between a man and a woman.
I want to sit down and start all over again,
Knowing this is wrong, that I'm in too deep.
And I want you to hear that if you're in a love so good,
At a time that's so wrong, let it go,
Because if it was truly meant to be it would come back to you.

I want everything in between,
But I can only have this,
The moment before the sun rises
And sometime after a full moon sets.

FALLING

In six months, three days and ten years
From now
I'll be writing on the wind.

In three years, six days and ten months
I'll be tiptoeing on water.

In ten days, three months and six years
You might just catch me flying with Jesus.

So until then,
Be sure to write on the wall of words.
Then I can know which message
To carry for you when you fall.

CAN I FADE WITH YOU?

I want to fade with you
Be that wilting flower at the end of June
Take the last rays of the sun
And go back to the dust where we belong.

I'd gladly accept my fate
If we could die together,
Hold each other
Without any thought of other beings.

I'd gladly take all of our memories
Fold them into my breast
And let them re grow into another life form
To hold and encapsulate a love that once existed, but wilted.

I'd gladly be that wilting flower,
Destroy those voices that can't understand
What it is to love
And write under noonday suns.

We'd smile with lollipops in our mouths
Run through the tall fields
With bare feet, un-calloused toes.

We'd touched the end of June
Stroke the last rays of the sun with our thoughts
Holding the beauty of Earth in our hands,
And spin each of the nine planets on our fingers.
We'd smile as we rotate beauty
Up into the sky,
Next to stars, suns and forgotten worlds
Allow it to spin its truths until we die.

For the last we'd spin together
Hold each other under cold moons
In chilly winds
To hide beneath leaves at night
Away from the spirits that haunt us.

Spirits that loom quietly over our souls
Commanding us to rejoin the children
Whose laughter reached up to the wilting flower of June.
If that flower died and the summer nights

Collapsed to the dead of winter
When the last angel has fallen,
Then I'd fade with you.

A BATTLE HE CAN WIN

His honey brown eyes stared down the universe with grief
He plagued his hands with tears and waited silently
As orchestrated death took everyone around him.
Silence rode his will hard, thundered through his soul with madness
And collapsed his heart strings to near defeat,
But still he rose with the pain that burdened his mind.

And so I climbed the peak to watch him reach
Heavens' pearly gates to avenge the death of his loved ones.
He was far gone from the place where two worlds meet in the sky.
As the war began between Heaven and Earth,
The stars began to fall with a burst of infinity.
The world was waiting for him to stand firm against Gabriel
And demand back the life that was taken.

His furrowed brow tightened the veins in his forehead
To staunch images of heroes fighting desperately for love.
His hands gripped the air around him to rip quickly through the clouds.
He soared towards the sun and eclipsed the moon.
It seemed the last days of heaven were here.
Finally the gods would rule the Earth no more.
Hercules would sing to the crowds that freedom had approached.

I watched him dance into heaven past the golden gates,
To regain the friends which left him, to see the family that loved him
And destroy the harps that lulled his children home.
I saw the wild destruction in his eyes,
As bursts of flames fell from the skies to the Earth.
For then I knew the dark days had come.

I urged him to end the raging madness in his heart,
But spare those who might be put in the dark by his fury,
Spare us for name sakes,
but destroy the iron chains placed on you by death.
Oh, how I knew, when our loves are lost to Death,
Their names are sung wildly in moans and cries
And their memories drowned in tears.

Oh, how I knew when love leaves here.
How Gabriel takes their souls to heaven's gates
Leaving us behind to live out our fates.
What comfort can I give to this man flying to the skies?
He has already become a ghost.

Katrice Williams

I wanted to tell him that we are pawns
In a chess game that can not leave.
We stand our ground and wait our fate,
Even a king too must wait.

My words were drowned as he battled on,
Silent to ears that would not listen.
Lost in eternity for a war that rages on.
He continues fighting there,
Waiting for his end.
Sending flames through fiery tears from the heavens,
He's become heaven's dark angel quietly awaiting
The day when love returns to him.

And I'll sit on this peak until there is a battle he can win.

THE MIAO WOMEN

Leaves fall from trees, float with the wind,
And intertwine their dead carcasses in the valley.
Blooming rice patties rise from the soil,
The leaves' nutrients spark a new future.
But what of the hands that plow
Or the women that labors with love
And only cares to be fed by the rice's grains?

What of their life?
What blessing do these women have?
Their voices stretched across the valley
Urging their husbands to come home,
Desperately trying to stop their children
From traveling after hopeless dreams.

Who is there to help the Miao woman,
Deep in the Chinese valley?
Her curved back of experience is soon battered
By hopelessness that these patties
Is all she'll ever know.

The deep night wraps its blanket around her,
But the moon meets her rising eyes
Instead of the sun.

She only weeps in childbirth.
After the third child she stops crying,
Only shifting to push the next baby out.
She settles on her bed for a few hours after,
Then returns to her plowing,
The newborn on her back,
Her daughters working and pulling beside her.

Her only son trots off to school in a land
Beyond the valley, the dirt roads, donkeys,
Rice patties and village life to
The grand cities with Mao upright and statuesque,
And to a place where few Miao men dare venture.

MONGOLIAN ANCESTORS

The twilight of dawn blinded my eyes,
No longer sheltering the day that took
Months to prepare for.
I traveled across the great American Terrain,
Pacific Ocean and mountains to reach China.

There I would meet the descendents of the Mongols,
Hui, Uygur, Miao, Yi and Manchu.
Names that twisted and writhed themselves from my tongue.
Languages that I'd never speak,
Only listen to in amazement as others translated our stories.

Stories that I wished to understand,
Could only be spoken with smiles as we ended our greetings
And then they turned back to implant their seeds,
Hoping their last wish for the rainy season
Would break the Chinese revolution.

A revolution that promised progress and change,
Only burdened them with Mao's uncompleted dreams.
Some of those dreams are still left as fragments
Of canals waiting to be built and bellies to be filled.
They're only half of the story he promised,
The rest told by the hands turned upwards to the heavens
Praying to their ancestors to bring them relief.
I heard the explosions in their hearts as no one heard their prayers.
I pleaded with the river to carry them to a better life.
I promised that I would not let their soul's fragments wash away.
I listened intently as I trekked through the valley.
It said the memories of their ancestors went up to the stars,
Giving the divine right to the emperor.
His highness had power to give silk and opium to foreigners,
But refused to listen to the revolt of his people.

They weren't Mandarin or Cantonese,
Just remnants of tribes left behind in his territory.
They're known as the nomadic people
Settled amongst poverty, ashes and mountains in Guizhou.
They're people who wipe their tears with dirty hands
And plant hopes in the running rivers…
I was only the girl with oak tree skin
Enveloping the Chinese flower of Li descent.
I walked on their thin lines of rice patties

And lied in the ashes left by communism.
I saw children walking barefoot on dying dreams of glass.

I know not how they balanced yesterday and tomorrow,
Their feet cut open by the lie that freedom was in the great cities
Away from the villages and thin patty lines.
I could not eat their crops or consume their traditions
I could only remember the hunch-backed woman
Wrapped in black cloth as I descended from the valley.
I left those patties and traveled back home on a mechanical bird.
The last thing I remembered,
Was a statue with an iron fist pressed to his heart,
And the one story of how…

Their dreams died with the red setting sun.

A LIST OF DREAMS

Ten years from now I will walk on water,
Form urban ghettoes out of sapphire cities
Underneath my feet.
I'll make Atlantis drink from the cups of griots,
recite poetry in ancient Egyptian temples
and then run naked after lion's hearts.

For the next ten years, pale-skinned, dark haired soldiers
from droplet-bending water kingdoms
will learn how to take sea spray,
and form an atlas of the earth redecorating
the night sky with patterns of land.

Dark-skinned, thick haired brothers
will tip the social scales back into balance,
the grain of woman
making all of the world's difference,
and tiny children will wring their fingers
together to sip tea with the uncrowned queen.

Eleven years from now,
I'll write poetry when I'm high
From incantations to the queen Nefertiti.
I'll sit meditating in the pharaoh's tomb,
by the golden-built guards and back-bending servants
who walked King Tutankhamen to the other side of Hades.
I'll write the four seasons for Helen and Troy,
when the north wind comes to capture iceberg blocs,
and the south wind comes to capture the heat
waves of sun-surfing Saturn storms,
the east wind comes to capture a taste of Mongolian rum,
and the west wind comes to bring a tsunami
to taste the fury of whirlwinds.

Twelve years from now my eyes
will fold back the anger
that has blinded me from blessing my enemies.

Thirteen years from now,
my hands will clothe the child of Zion
and dance with Mercedes
in song about the reproduction
of Karma and a middle earth peace

wave that has shocked the system of time.

Fourteen years from now
clocks will be off-schedule.
And transportation systems
will only run off the African saying
that the bus will move when it's full.

Fifteen years from now
colored people's time won't exist.
We'll laugh when hurried feet
try to catch a ball of cloud,
hoping they haven't missed the
reopening of the book of life.

Sixteen years from now,
I'll be in heaven with you,
sipping home-made lemonade
with a touch of sparkled-ice tea.
We'll think back and wonder
If we ever existed.

Seventeen years from now
I won't experience writer's block.

Eighteen years from now,
no one will need sleep,
only dreams.

Nineteen years from now,
I hope I will have finished this poem.

Twenty years from now
I'll hate writing narrative poems
about how you don't know me
and how I'm high off of incantations
writing the next list of dreams
for forty years, instead of three.

ON THE ROAD TO DAMASCUS

Children kick rocks in the dust
Around the woman who lies wrapped in the dirty, red cloth.
Sprawled, drunken and lost
She opens her eyes to the blazing sun.

The hazy white light in the middle
Of the Sahara desert darkens her skin to hazelnut.
She picks up arms, legs and feet
To begin the road to Damascus.

Her legs are scarred, but still she dances.
The only thing about her that remains beautiful,
Are the long, dark locks.

Her thoughts are scattered.
Wandering from Samaria by foot,
Every market, every struggle she dances in
Keeps her floating like the wind.
She doesn't know why she wanders.
Only that on the road to Damascus,
Hands promise her food, drink and love.

With every promise she is beaten.
She hopes that at the end of the road,
Her true value will be found,
That markets won't be empty when she dances,
That coins will fall at her feet,
Spinning to the ground as she spins.

She dances and listens to the light.
Speaking from the heavens,
Commanding her to move her shoulders,
Sway her arms, spin her hips, twirl her body,
And dance with her feet.

Pebbles glitter along the road,
Shards of glass that cut into her feet as she dances.
She can't see the eyes of camels,
Nomads slipping along in dark robes.
Her body just moves to the rhythm
Of the Congolese drum and the rumba.

She finds that the pebbles aren't pebbles,

But diamonds.

Gazing and staring at their glass fixture,
Her body begins to swirl the diamonds
Around her like a spiral as she dances.
The more she moves, the more the diamonds
Flow to her body's beat and
Form a halo around her head.
Dancing and swaying she moves along the road.
The more she sways, the more she gathers.
She has all she needs.

What music and dance does she need to play for passers-by?
What value can they give her?
What wisdom does she have that can't be found in her locks?
Keep dancing the light says.

"Move your feet as if there were no shackles,
Learn to dance in rhythm to the beat,
Rhythm and song of the road
that carries the diamonds of your worth."

On the road to Damascus,
The halo glitters for miles.
In day, it blinds the nomads.
At night, it blinds the stars.
A queen is dancing,
She is coming.

Be careful, she already knows her worth.

THE END

The end will never come unless we allow it.

My journey doesn't stop here,
It will always continue.

As long as you lift your wings,
My pen will keep writing.